BY NASA COMPUTER
KATHERINE JOHNSON
With her daughters Joylette Hylick and Katherine Moore

One Step
FURTHER

My Story of Math, the Moon, and a Lifelong Mission

Illustrations by Charnelle Pinkney Barlow

NATIONAL
GEOGRAPHIC
KiDS

Washington, D.C.

I'm Katherine Johnson.
Maybe you've heard of me: I helped send American astronauts into space and bring them safely home again.

Katherine Johnson with her girls in 1949. Pictured from left to right in front row: Connie, Katherine (Kathy), and Joylette

This is our story.

As a child, I loved numbers. And I loved to count. Every day, I counted the steps to school.

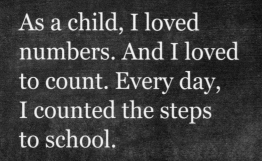

Katherine and her first husband, Jimmie Goble

My daughters, Joylette, Connie, and Kathy, loved to count, too.

Four plates. Three girls. Two churches on our street. One little white dog.

Math and music filled our home.

Jacks with onesie-twosies. Hopscotch: 1, 2, 3, 4. And piano. Music is like math. You count beats like you count numbers. One beat, two beats, three beats, four.

And love and learning filled our lives. Every Sunday we went to church. And every weekday the girls went to school. They counted each step as they went.

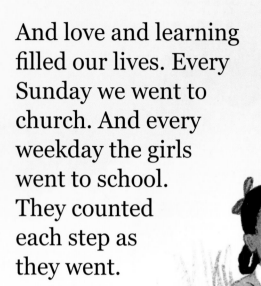

We all loved to learn. When Connie started school, I wanted to start school, too. I followed her, and the teacher let me stay!

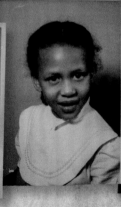

From left: Kathy (1st grade), Connie (1st grade), and Joylette (3rd grade)

There were things you could count— steps, plates, musical beats—and things you could count on. You could count on each other, family, and community.

But you could also count on life being hard.

In many places in the United States, it was against the law for Black people and white people to do things together. Black children couldn't go to school with white children. "Whites Only" and "Colored Only" signs hung on bathrooms and swimming pools.

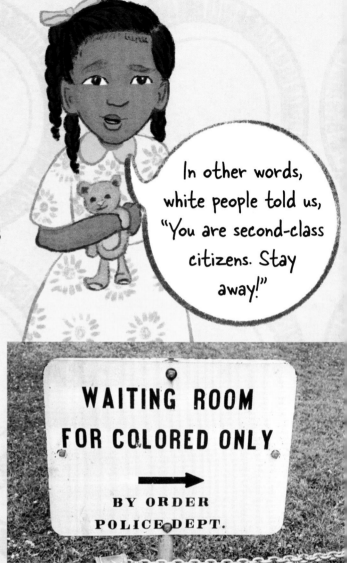

In other words, white people told us, "You are second-class citizens. Stay away!"

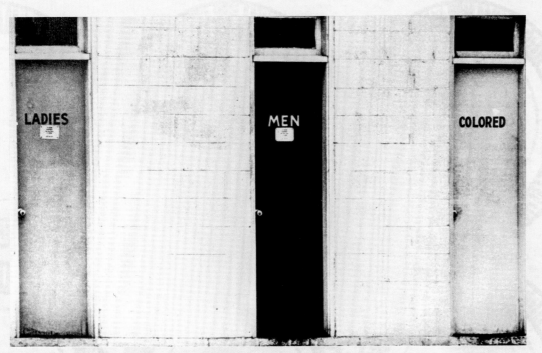

Laws, known as Jim Crow laws, kept Black people and white people separate. This was called segregation. Most of the time, the facilities provided for Black people were not as nice as the ones provided for white people.

Above: from left, Connie (age 5), Joylette (age 8), and Kathy (age 4); far right: the Coleman family home in White Sulphur Springs, West Virginia, where Katherine lived as a child and Kathy and Connie were born; right: Katherine's parents, Joshua and Joylette Coleman

But within our community, we were surrounded by our friends and family, who protected us from the scary world outside.

Colleges were kept separate, too. And it was difficult for many Black people to find the time or money to attend college at all. But I was lucky to be able to take that step. At college, I took a class about how the sun, moon, and stars move, and I earned a degree in math.

Even so, it was hard to find work. For many Black people, it was hard to find a job other than as a laborer, janitor, servant, or maid. But with my college degree, I was able to become a teacher. I said education was the key to equality.

Left: Katherine's report card, college graduation program, a press clipping, and a photo of Katherine and two classmates at their college graduation

I believed in teaching, and I believed in my students.
But Black teachers didn't earn a lot of money.
And it could be a dangerous job. Many white people
didn't want Black children to have an education, and
Black teachers and students were often threatened.

So my husband and I took a big step.
We moved our family to a new home
with more opportunities for work.

At Katherine's parents' home in White
Sulphur Springs at Christmas around
1951. Top: Katherine; second row, from
left: Katherine's father and mother
and Kathy (age 7); third row: Joylette
(age 11); bottom row: Connie (age 8)

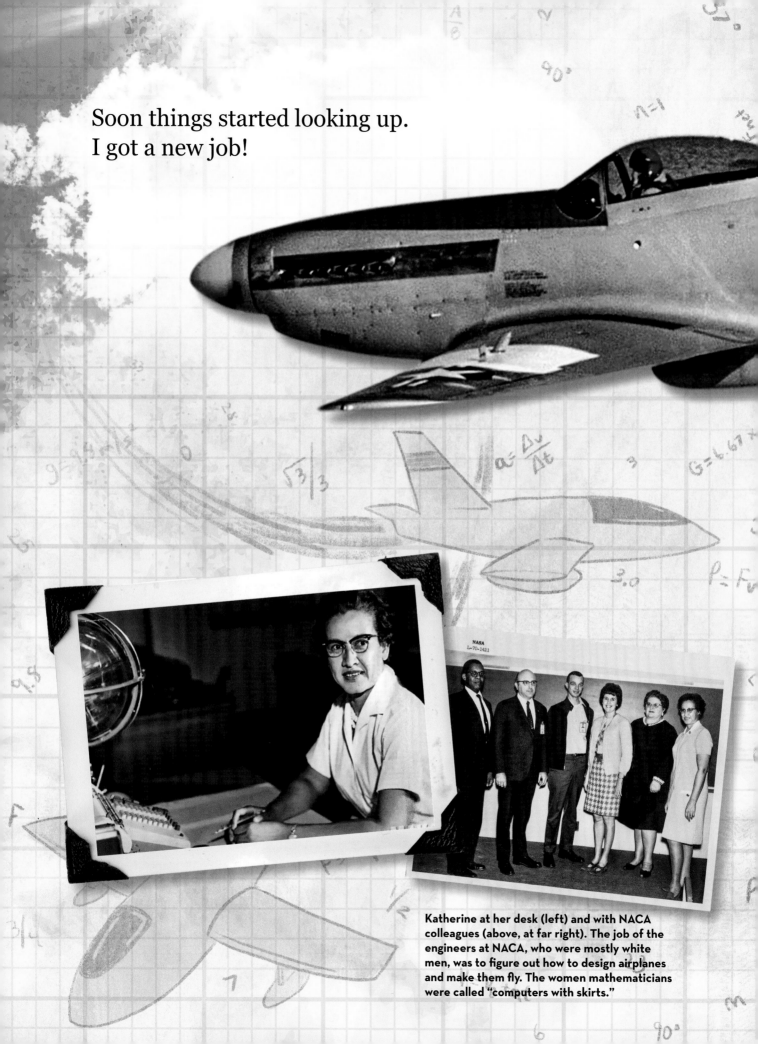

Soon things started looking up.
I got a new job!

Katherine at her desk (left) and with NACA colleagues (above, at far right). The job of the engineers at NACA, who were mostly white men, was to figure out how to design airplanes and make them fly. The women mathematicians were called "computers with skirts."

At the National Advisory Committee for Aeronautics (NACA), women were hired as computers. Back then, computers were people, not machines.

Engineers would ask important questions: Is the shape of this jet better? How can this plane fly farther?

Then human computers would calculate the answers.

On my first day, I picked out the perfect jacket and skirt, pearls and red lipstick, and I reported to work. I was amazed to see dozens of college-educated African-American women typing numbers into their calculating machines.

The sound of their click-click-clicking was like music. I took my seat and got to work.

Every morning, I carefully chose my clothes, put on my pearls and lipstick, and carpooled to work with other computers.

Our neighborhood was full of smart and stylish Black women mathematicians. At church, at school pickups, at summer cookouts, in our kitchen.

They took such pride in their jobs and looked so perfect every day. We didn't know quite what they did, but we wanted to be like them.

We felt we needed to be perfect: We needed to dress perfectly, act perfectly, and do perfect work. Even though most of us had college degrees and had earned high grades, the truth was that white people thought we weren't as smart as they were, just because of the color of our skin.

I saw this kind of discrimination everywhere around me. Black people had to work twice as hard to be thought of as half as good as white people. It made me so mad.

☑ Arrive on time
☑ Nice clothes
☑ Perfect hair
☑ Complete all work

And just as there was segregation outside of the workplace, Black computers worked in an entirely separate area of the NACA campus. Even the bathrooms and cafeterias were separate.
I chose to eat at my desk instead.

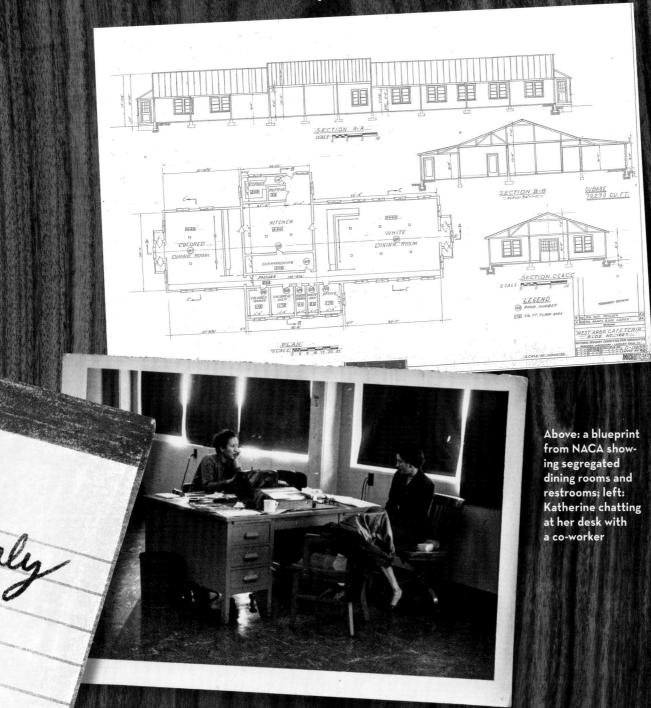

Above: a blueprint from NACA showing segregated dining rooms and restrooms; left: Katherine chatting at her desk with a co-worker

I never missed a day of work. I loved the math.
But even more, I loved asking questions.
Most computers just calculated math problems.
But I wanted to know *how* the math was being
used. I wanted to know *why*.

White men weren't used to a Black woman
questioning them. Some were angry.
But I kept asking. Understanding why the numbers
were needed helped me do my best work.

One day, I went one step further.
I asked, "Can I come to meetings?"
The answer was no. Women, and especially
computers, weren't allowed at meetings.
"Is there a law against it?" I asked.
I got to go to meetings after that.

Soon, NACA had a new name—
NASA—and a new mission:
sending humans into space!
It was something the United
States hadn't done before.
Much of my new work was
secret. I couldn't talk
about it at home.

From left: Connie
(7th grade), Joylette
(10th grade), and
Kathy (7th grade)

As my career grew, so did my daughters. At college, Kathy was helping her country take a step further—toward equality. In Greensboro, North Carolina, she and other Black students and adults such as ministers were peacefully protesting to change laws and to end racial segregation.

Ministers protesting segregated lunch counters in 1960

We marched through downtown, two by two. We held sit-ins at "Whites Only" lunch counters. White people spit and threw water and popcorn on us.

I prayed for Kathy's safety, but I was so proud of her. She was doing important work to help our country. I kept working to help our country, too. Every day, I worked out math problems. I asked questions. I knew my equations and questions would help our country take step after step as we tried to send a human into space.

Soon, NASA chose John Glenn, Jr., to be the first American who would not just fly into space, but also circle Earth! It was a dangerous mission, and there was a lot at stake.

Astronaut John Glenn, Jr. (left and right), trains for his upcoming spaceflight.

As they prepared to send Glenn into orbit, NASA brought in a new kind of computer—a machine. The machines were much faster at math than humans. But were they as good at the math? Would their calculations be correct?

Many at NASA didn't trust the machines. Unlike human computers, machines didn't ask questions. They didn't understand the math. They just calculated numbers.

As blastoff day neared, John Glenn made an urgent request. He wanted me to check the machine's math. He would not take off until I did.

I worked for two full days to double-check the machine's math. Every number counted.

Finally my calculations were done, and Glenn stepped into the spacecraft. He blasted off into space, circled three times around the planet, then splashed down safely back on Earth.

John Glenn, Jr., enters his spacecraft, Friendship 7, before blasting off.

Sending a human into orbit around Earth was a great accomplishment, but soon the United States would take a step that no one had done before: They would put a human on the moon!

It was one thing to reach the moon. NASA knew how to do that. They had already sent an uncrewed spacecraft there. It was another thing to send astronauts to the moon and bring them back home safely.

The answer was in the math that moved the sun, moon, and stars. So I asked more questions.

What direction is the world spinning? At what time must we launch?

My questions helped
the scientists figure out
what calculations needed
to be made. If the math
was wrong, the spacecraft
would miss the moon.
This time, no one
questioned my questions.
I got to work.

On July 16, 1969, the whole world counted
down from ten to one and watched as
Neil Armstrong, Buzz Aldrin, and
Mike Collins rocketed into space.

From left: Neil Armstrong,
Mike Collins, and
Buzz Aldrin

I counted down, too.
TEN. NINE. EIGHT.
SEVEN. SIX. FIVE.
FOUR. THREE.
TWO. ONE ...

BLASTOFF!

Buzz Aldrin after planting the U.S. flag on the moon

Now, everyone on the planet asked the same questions: Would they make it to the moon? And, would they make it back home again?

I was studying in the library a few days later when I saw Mom's picture in a newspaper. I shouted, "That's my mother!"

The Daily Post

LADY MATHEMATICIAN SENDS MAN TO MOON

The rest, as they say, is history.

The click-clack of computing machines became like music to me.

Joylette followed in her mother's footsteps and worked at NASA. She later completed a master's degree, taking her education and her career one step further than her mother's.

Kathy followed in her mother's footsteps by becoming a teacher. She received a master's degree and spent 33 years as a public schoolteacher and guidance counselor.

In every student, I saw a future educator, mathematician, astronaut.

Connie became a teacher as well. Like her mother, she felt that teaching children was a calling. Connie also drove a giant truck and did landscaping and wallpapering! She passed away in 2010.

Katherine retired from NASA in 1986. When she was 97 years old, NASA named a building after her. When she was 100, NASA named an entire facility after her.

Decades before, when she had joined NASA, no one could have imagined such a thing. But Katherine had gazed into space and studied its math. She'd asked questions and gone to work.

Racial Segregation in the United States

Centuries ago, many Africans were kidnapped from their homes and forcibly brought to North America as slaves. The first documented instance of enslaved people being transported to the English colonies in North America was in Jamestown, Virginia, in 1619. Though slavery was ended in 1865, African Americans have struggled to attain freedom and equality in the United States ever since.

A few decades after the U.S. Civil War, which helped give African Americans their formal, legal freedom, a series of laws, known as Jim Crow laws, were put into place. These laws aimed to keep Black people separated from white people, and they permitted the unfair, often terrible, treatment of Black people. This included separate water fountains, entrances and waiting rooms, schools, restrooms, and more. Signs posted at each of these locations indicated which were "Whites Only" and which were "Colored Only." For Katherine Johnson, this meant that her family lived in African-American communities and attended African-American-only churches and schools. Black people were paid much less than white people

for doing the same job, and when Katherine went to work at NACA, the African-American computers sat in a completely different area from the white computers. In fact, at first, many white computers were not even aware of the African-American computers!

By the 1960s, there was growing pressure for change, and the civil rights movement was in full swing. This movement worked to end racial segregation and ensure equality for

African Americans. Many different leaders brought many different tactics to the movement. Nonviolent civil disobedience was one particularly effective method. When practicing civil disobedience, people calmly and politely break a law that they feel is unfair. They try to avoid any kind of violence—they just *disobey* the law. In Greensboro, North Carolina, in 1960, a group of Black students began a kind of civil disobedience called a sit-in. The students went to Whites Only lunch counters and sat on the stools. They knew they wouldn't be served food, but they wanted to bring attention to the unfairness of the law that forced them to eat at Colored Only lunch counters. While the protesters were often treated harshly, their civil disobedience worked, and soon some lunch counters began to allow Black people and white people to eat together.

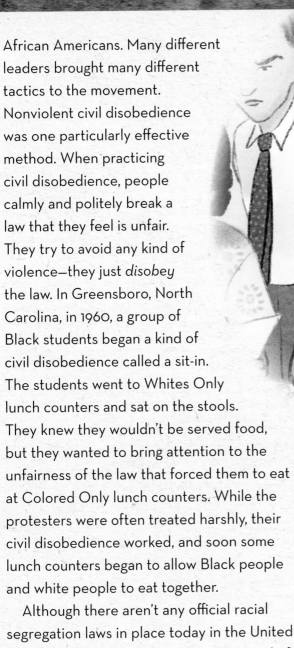

Although there aren't any official racial segregation laws in place today in the United States, many groups of people still struggle for equality both in the United States and around the world. Women are often paid less than men for doing the same job. Many minorities struggle to have access to the same resources as others. But there are also many people still fighting for equal rights. Though progress may be slow, each small step brings equality for all that much closer to reality.

About Katherine Johnson

On August 26, 1918, Katherine Coleman was born the youngest of four children to Joshua and Joylette Coleman. From the time she was young, she enjoyed numbers and counting and arranging things. This didn't surprise either of her parents—before Katherine was born, her mother had been a schoolteacher and her father could tell how many logs a tree would produce just by looking at it.

Joshua and Joylette Coleman fought for their children's education. Back then, an education wasn't guaranteed to every child in the United States. In fact, it was rare for the education of an African-American child to extend past the eighth grade. Politicians passed a law barring Black students from attending the only high school in the Colemans' hometown of White Sulphur Springs, West Virginia. As with most cities in America during the first half of the 20th century, the high school in White Sulphur Springs was for white children only. Refusing to let their children go without an education, Joshua and Joylette relocated their family to Institute, West Virginia, during the school year. There, the children could attend the West Virginia State College (now West Virginia State University), which offered high school and college-level courses. Unable to find a job in the area, Joshua continued to live in White Sulphur Springs, visiting with his family when he could.

Katherine went on to earn her bachelor's degree in mathematics and French from West Virginia State College in 1937. She earned the highest grade-point average attained by any student in the history of the college. She then began a graduate program as one of the first three African Americans to ever attend the previously all-white West Virginia University, though she chose not to complete the program.

Because her career options were limited by her race and gender, Katherine began

Left: Katherine, at age 2 (seated, bottom left) with her sister, Margaret, and brothers Charles and Horace; right: Katherine (next to last in line) with her parents and siblings

her career teaching math, French, and music to Black children. Back then, teaching Black children was a dangerous career choice. Many white people believed that educating African-American people would cause them to challenge their "place" in society. These people worried that African Americans would want better jobs and higher pay. Across the American South, a group called the Ku Klux Klan (KKK) burned many schools down and terrorized African-American teachers and others.

In 1952, Katherine and her husband James "Jimmie" Goble moved their family to Newport News, Virginia. Jimmie found higher-paying work in the shipyards there. Katherine applied to NACA that same year, but she was turned down—she was told that NACA had already met its quota for Black employees and would not be hiring more until the next year. Katherine returned the following year and was finally hired and able to begin her work with NACA (later NASA).

At NASA, Katherine calculated the flight path for astronaut Alan Shepard, Jr.'s historic spaceflight on May 5, 1961. Shepard was the first American to fly in space.

Katherine is perhaps best known, however, for responding to astronaut John Glenn, Jr.'s last-minute request that she double-check the new IBM computer's calculations for his orbit of planet Earth in 1962. He would not take off until she did so. "If she says they're good," he said, "then I am ready to go." Glenn's trip marked a pivotal moment for the United States in the Space Race.

Katherine also calculated two possible orbits for the first crewed trip to the moon in July 1969. This included calculating the azimuth, or the point in the flight where the process of bringing the spacecraft back down to Earth begins. She also worked on the space shuttle program and co-authored 26 research reports, including the first report in her division that gave author credit to a woman.

In 2015, Katherine was awarded the Presidential Medal of Freedom, the nation's most prestigious civilian honor. The following year, NASA honored her legacy by naming a building after her: the Katherine G. Johnson Computational Research Facility, and in 2019, NASA renamed several buildings as the Katherine Johnson Independent Verification and Validation (IV&V) Facility.

Katherine died in 2020 at the age of 101.

August 26, 1918 Katherine Coleman is born in White Sulphur Springs, West Virginia.

1929 At the age of 10, Katherine starts high school at West Virginia State College, a high school and college for African-American students.

1937 Katherine graduates from the West Virginia State College (later renamed West Virginia State University) at the age of 18, with a degree in math and French.

1939 Katherine marries James "Jimmie" Goble.

December 27, 1940 Joylette Goble is born.

April 27, 1943 Constance "Connie" Goble is born. She died in 2010.

April 17, 1944 Katherine "Kathy" Goble is born.

1952 The Gobles relocate to Newport News, Virginia.

1953 Katherine gets a job at NACA (later NASA).

May 17, 1954 In the landmark case *Brown* v. *Board of Education of Topeka, Kansas,* the Supreme Court of the United States rules that racial segregation of children in public schools is unconstitutional.

December 1, 1955 Seamstress and civil rights activist Rosa Parks refuses to give up her seat on a Montgomery, Alabama, bus, sparking the Montgomery bus boycott. This strike by African-American passengers proved pivotal in the civil rights movement.

December 20, 1956 Jimmie Goble dies.

October 4, 1957 The Soviet Union launches the Sputnik satellite, the first object to be placed in Earth's orbit, a major milestone in the Space Race.

1958 Joylette graduates with honors from George W. Carver High School and attends Hampton Institute (later renamed Hampton University).

1958 NACA is renamed NASA, the National Aeronautics and Space Administration.

August 22, 1959 Katherine Coleman Goble marries James Johnson, changing her name to Katherine Johnson.

May 5, 1961 Supported by calculations made by Katherine Johnson, astronaut Alan Shepard, Jr., becomes the first American in space, traveling approximately 300 miles in 15 minutes.

May 25, 1961 President John F. Kennedy declares that the United States will catch up to the Soviets in the Space Race and land an astronaut on the moon by the end of the decade.

1961 Connie and Kathy graduate from George W. Carver High School. Connie goes on to attend and graduate from Hampton Institute. Kathy attends

Bennett College, but later transfers and also graduates from Hampton Institute.

February 20, 1962 Astronaut John Glenn, Jr., becomes the first person to successfully orbit Earth, an almost five-hour flight circling Earth three times—but not before "the girl" checked the IBM computer's calculations. Although Glenn did not acknowledge Katherine Johnson by name, she was well known throughout the flight mechanics department responsible for flight oversight.

1962 Joylette graduates from Hampton Institute with a bachelor's degree in mathematics and begins working as a computer at NASA.

August 28, 1963 More than 260,000 Americans participate in the March on Washington for Jobs and Freedom in Washington, D.C., where civil rights leader Dr. Martin Luther King, Jr., delivers his famous "I Have a Dream" speech.

November 22, 1963 President John F. Kennedy is assassinated and Vice President Lyndon B. Johnson becomes president.

January 1964 Joylette leaves NASA to move to New Jersey. Her husband, also a graduate of Hampton Institute, had been denied employment as a Black accountant in the segregated South.

July 2, 1964 President Lyndon B. Johnson signs the Civil Rights Act of 1964, making segregation illegal in public spaces and prohibiting employment discrimination on the basis of race, color, religion, sex, or national origin, including at courthouses, parks, restaurants, theaters, sports arenas, and hotels. Later, the law was expanded to include physically challenged and older people, and then women playing sports in college.

August 6, 1965 President Lyndon B. Johnson signs the National Voting Rights Act of 1965, banning the use of racial tactics—including poll taxes, constitutional knowledge tests, birth certificates, and other strategies designed to keep African-American people from voting—and authorizing the U.S. attorney general to investigate efforts to prevent Black people from voting.

April 4, 1968 Dr. Martin Luther King, Jr., is assassinated in Memphis, Tennessee, while leading the "Poor People's Campaign," a multiracial movement made up of low-income Americans fighting for economic justice. He was also speaking out against the Vietnam War.

April 11, 1968 President Lyndon B. Johnson signs the Fair Housing Act of 1968, making it unlawful for people who are selling, renting, or financing a home to discriminate based on race, religion, national origin, or gender.

July 16, 1969 The Apollo 11 spaceflight takes off. Four days later, on July 20, the first humans—astronauts Neil Armstrong and Edwin "Buzz" Aldrin, supported by astronaut Michael Collins—land on the moon.

1986 Katherine Johnson retires from NASA after 33 years of calculating flight trajectories and orbits for numerous space missions and working on the space shuttle program.

1998 Katherine receives her first honorary doctorate degree from State University of New York at Farmingdale.

2015 President Barack Obama awards Katherine Johnson with the Presidential Medal of Freedom, the highest civilian honor bestowed by a U.S. president.

2016 The book *Hidden Figures* and the movie by the same name are released.

2017 The Katherine G. Johnson Computational Research Facility at NASA's Langley Research Center opens.

August 26, 2018 Katherine celebrates her 100th birthday.

March 13, 2019 Katherine's husband, James Johnson, dies in Newport News, Virginia.

April 2019 Katherine receives her 13th honorary degree, a doctorate from the University of Johannesburg, South Africa.

July 2019 NASA names the Katherine Johnson Independent Verification and Validation (IV&V) Facility.

November 2019 The U.S. Congress passes bipartisan legislation to honor Katherine with a Congressional Gold Medal.

February 24, 2020 Katherine dies at the age of 101.

GLOSSARY

Beat. In music, a beat is a regular pulse or pattern. If you're nodding your head, tapping your toes, or snapping your fingers to music you like, you're probably doing it to the beat.

Calculation. Whether you add, subtract, multiply, or divide, when you figure out a math problem, you've performed a calculation. For example, to know what time you need to leave home to get to school on time, you might calculate how long it will take you to brush your teeth, make your bed, get dressed, and eat breakfast, so you know what time to wake up.

Engineer. Engineers use science and math to design or make things.

NACA. The National Advisory Committee for Aeronautics. NACA was founded on March 3, 1915, to help the United States catch up to the Europeans in airplane research and technology. NACA was located at the Langley Memorial Aeronautical Laboratory at Langley Field in Hampton, Virginia.

NASA. On July 29, 1958, President Eisenhower signed the National Aeronautics and Space Act into law. Just two months later, on October 1, 1958, the National Advisory Committee for Aeronautics (NACA) was absorbed into the new agency the Space Act had formed: the National Aeronautics and Space Administration, or NASA. NASA was responsible for the nation's human, satellite, and robotic space programs, as well as aeronautical research. One of its earliest goals was to launch a space vehicle into orbit with a human aboard. Then, the goal was to put a human on the moon.

Racial segregation. After slavery was ended in the United States, the federal government, as well as many states, cities, and towns, passed laws, known as Jim Crow laws, that were unfair to African Americans. Their goal was to keep African Americans as second-class citizens. Though enacted throughout the United States, these laws and customs that separated people by race were particularly common throughout the South. Often these laws were accompanied by violent acts committed by white people to terrorize African Americans. Even though slavery had been abolished, these practices often forced African Americans to work for no or low wages and to be treated as unequal to white people.

Sit-in. A sit-in is a way of peacefully protesting. During a sit-in, protesters enter a public place, sit down, and, though remaining peaceful, refuse to leave until their concerns are addressed or they are removed by force. The methods used to remove the protesters are often violent.

Soviet Union. Between 1922 and 1991, a large nation named the Union of Soviet Socialist Republics—also called the U.S.S.R., or Soviet Union—formed in Eastern Europe and across northern Asia. The Soviet Union was made up of 15 republics—including nations that we today know as Russia, Armenia, Georgia, Ukraine, and others—and covered one-sixth of Earth's land area. Following World War II, the U.S.S.R. became the United States' primary political and economic rival.

Space Race. After World War II ended, the United States and the Soviet Union competed both in exploring outer space and in trying to be the first and the best in all stages of spaceflight. This included putting artificial satellites, uncrewed space probes, and flights crewed by humans into space. The race began in 1955, when both nations announced their plans to put satellites in orbit. On October 4, 1957, the Soviet Union launched its satellite first. Afraid that the Soviets might spy on the United States—or worse, use a satellite or spacecraft to drop a bomb—the United States hurried to catch up. Early the next year, the United States launched its first satellite. In 1961, President Kennedy announced that the United States would be the first to put humans on the moon. After a series of exploratory efforts—including attempts to reach outer space and orbit Earth—the Apollo 11 mission landed there on July 20, 1969. When the first humans landed on the moon, America claimed the Space Race title. Katherine Johnson was involved in these efforts.

As a child, I remember staring up at the night sky as we drove home from a holiday family get-together. The air was crisp (as was the norm for a New York winter) and the stars were bright. I looked up at the brightest star in the sky and wondered what its name was. I even made up some elaborate story in my head about the star's origin. I never imagined the time, dedication, and work that women like Katherine Johnson put into answering all the questions that could arise when NASA prepared to venture into this same night sky.

When I began creating the illustrations for this book, I wanted to acknowledge and celebrate the role that Katherine had in inspiring and leading her daughters to go one step further. Throughout the book, we get to see how each move Katherine made was a stepping-stone for them. One major task I had as the illustrator was to show Katherine, Joylette, Connie, and Kathy at different parts of their lives while still enabling readers to distinguish them from each other and recognize them as the same characters. One way this was accomplished was through clothing patterns (particularly for Katherine's daughters).

The design of the book inspired me, too. I love seeing how the illustrations interact with the photographs on each page. Being able to trace the family's journey through photography as well as illustration helped me put everything into context.

Even though Katherine Johnson wasn't a name mentioned in my history classes growing up, her story is one that should be told in every household. It was her love of questions and numbers that helped a human travel safely to space and back. I am honored to have a hand in sharing another side of her story that shows her influence on the generations of future mathematicians that came after her.

—*Charnelle Pinkney Barlow, Illustrator*

In the summer of 2019, I had the honor of being welcomed into the private home of Katherine Johnson. She was a celebrity, but she was a stranger to me, known only from a distance through books and the popular movie *Hidden Figures*.

As I sat on the floor of the spare bedroom of her home, sifting through shoeboxes, file folders, and thick family albums, it struck me that there's a reason why we call them personal items. These church programs, newspaper clippings, and photos have the ability to help bring a person's story to life, to make emotional connections. As I pored over school papers, sheet music, awards, and stacks of photos, Joylette and Kathy told me stories about each item—who *that* person was, and where *that* event took place, and what *that* award was for. They were generous with their time and opened up to me about what it was like growing up during the civil rights movement. With each item I photographed, I was getting closer and closer to all of the women in this book. I held in my hand Katherine's report card (so many A's!), her college diploma, her string of pearls, her Presidential Medal of Freedom. These are items only someone very close would ever have the privilege of touching. By the time I left, I felt like I was leaving the home of a neighbor and friend.

By including some of these incredibly personal photos and artifacts in our book, I hope that readers have the same experience and walk away caring more about these women and their mission to take one step further.

—Lori Epstein, Photo Director, National Geographic Kids Books

All original artwork by Charnelle Pinkney Barlow unless otherwise noted below.

GI: Getty Images; NGP: National Geographic Partners; SS: Shutterstock

Cover (rocket), NASA; (moon), NASA/Goddard/Lunar Reconnaissance Orbiter; (starry sky), Beautiful landscape/SS; back cover: (starry sky), Beautiful landscape/SS; (family photos), Lori Epstein/NGP; (photo corners), Brian A Jackson/SS; (floating numbers), Valentin Drull/SS; flap (UP), Lori Epstein/NGP; (LO), Charnelle Pinkney Barlow; 2 (rocket), NASA; 4, Lori Epstein/NGP; 6 (UP), Lori Epstein/NGP; 6 (plates), Smithsonian Institution; 6 (butterfly), Butterfly Hunter/SS; 6 (dog), trang trinh/SS; 6 (blackboard), K Woodgyer/SS; 7 (jacks), Photodisc; 7 (dominoes), DR Travel Photo and Video/SS; 7 (music notes), Igor/SS; 7 (numbers), Bernhard Schimmel/SS; 7 (hopscotch), Kirstin Mckee/Stocksy; 8, Lori Epstein/NGP; 10 (LE), Hulton Archive/GI; 10 (UP RT), William Lovelace/Express/Hulton Archive/GI; 10 (LO RT), PhotoQuest/GI; 11 (UP), Hulton Archive/GI; 11 (CTR LE, CTR RT & LO), Lori Epstein/NGP; 12 (UP, LO LE, CTR, & LO), Lori Epstein/NGP; 12 (LE), blackred/iStockphoto/GI; 13 (UP), Alfonso de Tomas/SS; 13 (LO), Mega/SS; 14, Lori Epstein/NGP; 16-17, NASA; 16 (LO LE & LO RT), NASA; 16-17 (sunny sky), 99Art/SS; (clouds in sky), kzww/SS; 17, NASA; 18 (UP), Lori Epstein/NGP; 18 (CTR), NASA; 18 (LO), Ingram; 21 (UP), NASA; 21 (LO), Lori Epstein/NGP; 24, Lori Epstein/NGP; 26, Everett/SS; 28 (LE & RT), NASA; 31, NASA; 34 (INSET), NASA; (rocket), NASA; 35, NASA; 40 (LE & RT), Lori Epstein/NGP; 42 (UP LE), Lori Epstein/NGP; 42 (LO LE), Bettmann/GI; 42 (UP RT), Everett/SS; 42 (LO RT), Lori Epstein/NGP; 43 (LE), Hulton Archive/GI; 43 (RT), AP Photo; 44 (ALL), Lori Epstein/NGP; 46, Jerry Pinkney; various pages and endsheets (lined & graph papers), filo/iStockphoto; (photo corners), Brian A Jackson/SS; (starry night sky), Beautiful landscape/SS; (blue watercolor paper), paladin13/GI; (speech balloons), Limbach/SS; (water-colored starry sky), Khaneeros/SS; (rocket on endsheet), Sergey Nivens/SS

In memory of my daughter Connie and in honor of the G-6 (my grandchildren), the delight of my life.

To all the children of the world, dream big and believe anything is possible.

—Katherine Johnson

Acknowledgments

The authors and publisher wish to thank the dedicated team that contributed to the creation of this book: Hilary Beard, for bringing her deep knowledge, attention to sensitivity, and passion to the text; Amy Novesky, for adding her magic touch to the text; Scott Vehstedt, for his careful and thorough fact-checking; and the National Geographic team that brought the book together: Shelby Lees, senior editor; Lori Epstein, photo director; Eva Absher-Schantz, art director and vice president, Kids Visual Identity; Joan Gossett, editorial production manager; and Anne LeongSon and Gus Tello, design production assistants.

Since 1888, the National Geographic Society has funded more than 12,000 research, exploration, and preservation projects around the world. The Society receives funds from National Geographic Partners, LLC, funded in part by your purchase. A portion of the proceeds from this book supports this vital work. To learn more, visit natgeo.com/info.

For more information, visit nationalgeographic.com, call 1-877-873-6846, or write to the following address:

National Geographic Partners
1145 17th Street N.W.
Washington, DC 20036-4688 U.S.A.

For librarians and teachers:
nationalgeographic.com/books/librarians-and-educators

More for kids from National Geographic: natgeokids.com

National Geographic Kids magazine inspires children to explore their world with fun yet educational articles on animals, science, nature, and more. Using fresh storytelling and amazing photography, *Nat Geo Kids* shows kids ages 6 to 14 the fascinating truth about the world—and why they should care. kids.nationalgeographic.com/subscribe

For rights or permissions inquiries, please contact National Geographic Books Subsidiary Rights: bookrights@natgeo.com

Designed by Eva Absher-Schantz

Hardcover ISBN: 978-1-4263-7193-6
Reinforced library binding ISBN: 978-1-4263-7194-3

Printed in Canada
20/FC/1